My Child Listen to Rock Music?

AL MENCONI

LIFEJOURNEY
BOOKS

LifeJourney Books is an imprint of David C. Cook
Publishing Co.
David C. Cook Publishing Co., Elgin, Illinois 60120
David C. Cook Publishing Co., Weston, Ontario
Nova Distribution, Ltd., Torquay, England

Should My Child Listen to Rock Music?
©1991 by Al Menconi
(This booklet consists of selected portions of *Today's
Music: A Window to Your Child's Soul* ©1990 by Al
Menconi with Dave Hart)

Edited by Brian Reck
Cover design by Bob Fuller
First printing, 1991
Printed in the United States of America
95 94 93 92 91   5 4 3 2 1

Library of Congress Cataloging in Publication Data

Menconi, Al
Should My Child Listen to Rock Music?
Al Menconi
     p. cm. — (Helping Families Grow series)
ISBN: 1-55513-659-1
1. Rock music—Religious aspects—Christianity.
I. Title.   II. Series:
ML3534.M49   1991
241'.652—dc20   91-26986
                                 CIP

"A mirror reflects a man's face, but what he is really like is shown by the kind of friends he chooses" (Proverbs 27:19, TLB).

Almost every day our office receives letters and phone calls asking for a list of all the "bad rock groups" or the "satanic rock bands." Without a proper understanding of young people and their music, such facts can become clubs with which adults try to beat their children into submission. It is not our desire to provide weapons or ammunition that will add to an already tense situation. We would rather provide effective tools for enhancing communication with your children.

The complex problem of contemporary music in today's Christian family has no simple, one-step solutions. Today's music involves so much more than just Satanism. Theories about demon beats and backmasking are speculative at best. They may be fascinating, but few people are really motivated to sincere, lasting changes for Jesus because of such arguments. And trying to force our children to like what we like is not usually constructive, either.

Perhaps the most misleading idea is believing that a direct cause-and-effect relationship exists between music and a child's behavior. We desperately want to blame music for all the dramatic and destructive changes in our children.

Some people teach that rock music is the primary reason for teenage drug and alcohol abuse, pregnancies, suicides, and Satan worship. These people conclude that if we could just remove the bad musical influences from young lives, all the problems would disappear as well. Then their children could get on with living wholesome and holy lives. Thus parenting is reduced to a simple formula: remove the music, get the kid saved, and everything will be all right.

Obviously, these people have never been parents! Theirs would be a wonderfully convenient solution, if it only worked. But it is quite simplistic and naive. The theory sounds fine until it is actually applied in a real, live family. Then it splits parents and young people and pushes them to opposite extremes of the music spectrum.

At one end are the adults whose arguments just do not hold up given the variables of peer pressure, education, divorce, the family's spiritual condition, the parent/child relationship, or physical/emotional changes that come from simply growing up. These are all important elements in a child's development that cannot be ignored.

At the other end of the spectrum are the equally naive young people who claim that music is not the problem. In fact, they say music has absolutely no effect on them. This claim is also simplistic and short-sighted. Music may not be the *only* influence in our children's lives, but it is certainly a *powerful* one.

As is often the case, the truth lies somewhere between the two extremes. Music may indeed influence our children over time. But it does not work like black magic nor should it be completely ignored.

Before we can move on to the practical "how to's" of dealing with rock music in our homes and churches, we should first consider one more concept that can resolve the conflict and eliminate the misunderstanding between the two extremes. It is the key to success in dealing with today's music. If properly understood, this concept can bring back communication, unity, and spiritual health to our families.

IN SEARCH OF CLUES

Our hope lies in realizing that we can use music as a *clue* rather than a *club*. A young person's music is deeply personal to him, so it is almost impossible to condemn the music without making the child feel rejected as well. Our children don't feel that we are attacking some external evil called music. They feel that we are attacking them personally. If we get drawn into this kind of struggle, it will always prove to be a losing battle. Not only will we end up losing the music war, but we may end up losing our children as well.

So how can we use music as a clue? By listening closely to a child's music, we can discover what our children really feel, what they believe, what they like, and what they need. But isn't their music providing worldly advice to problems that need spiritual answers? Of course it is. But if we will take a moment to think this through, we get to the source of the real problem: our children's empty hearts.

There are a number of music styles that are popular with young people today. Each of these styles provides clues to our children's inner worlds if we will only take a little time to listen and think. Let's now look at how you can use these clues to discover how this music can be a window to *your* child's soul.

Clues from Dark Music

The somber and pessimistic viewpoint of dark music (new wave, alternative, new rock) seems to appeal to the more intellectual, introspective, and passive teen. The music focuses on broken hearts, hurt feelings, and all the things that are wrong with the world. Some of these musical observations may be accurate. We *are* surrounded by war, corruption, foolishness, and selfishness. But the problem with dark music is that it rarely offers an answer. According to these artists, the world is bleak and we have no choice but to sit and stare at the wall, waiting for the end.

Fans of this music tend to think too much and take too little action. They have given up and given in to listless apathy. Their claim that there are no solutions is often a coverup for poor self-esteem. They feel hopeless, helpless, and inadequate to achieve the kinds of changes they wish they could make. Dark music about an ugly world fits their inner feelings of personal ugliness and worthlessness.

This kind of young person often has too much: too much time, too much money, too much intelligence. We need to offer this type of child goals that will give him a sense of purpose and self-worth. We need to help provide him with a deeper realization of his true value in Christ's sight. He needs to experience a sense of meaning through the accomplishment of successful changes in his immediate world.

Clues from Hard Rock/Heavy Metal

The high energy and colorful image of party metal and hard rock lead many young people to believe that this music can help them escape the rigors of responsibility and the painful side of life. According to the messages in this music, love is always just around the corner and the party never ends.

Party metal fans are often looking for validation, excitement, and acceptance by their peers because they don't believe it lies within themselves. The answer must be somewhere "out there," around the corner, in the future. Unsure of themselves, they tend to blame everyone and everything else. They frequently admit to not liking or trusting their present circumstances or environment.

These young people will learn that the party always ends and there are always dues to pay. Perhaps we can guide them to this knowledge sooner, rather than later. We can't always help young people avoid the consequences of their choices. But we *can* pray that we will be there by their sides when disaster strikes. With wisdom, we can use these teachable, vulnerable moments to show them that their music lied to them. But more than this, we need to affirm that value and security are theirs already—in their family, in their circumstances, and in themselves as unique and special creations of God.

Black metal fans may also be looking for an escape, but their needs tend to be deeper and darker. This music is based on power and revenge. It offers solutions in black magic which promise the ability to protect oneself, to receive rewards, to accomplish great deeds, and to wreak havoc on enemies. This music appeals to the teen who feels life is out of control or who has been deeply hurt. Sometimes it reflects a cry of anger against a Christian religion that is strangling the would-be sorcerer.

Adults need to look beyond the music to the potentially traumatic events in the lives of these listeners. What has caused so much fear and rage in their souls? Perhaps deaths, divorces, abuses, or suicides? God understands this kind of severe pain. He felt it when His Son died. He also knows how to forgive and help a person begin again.

The crudeness and violence of thrash metal might be repulsive to an adult, but it can be very reassuring to an angry adolescent who feels that his world is out of control. Many fans feel inadequate, frustrated, and angry. And perhaps they have good reason to feel the way they do, such as an alcoholic parent, a lack of communication in the family, a divorce in the home, or some other unavoidable situation. Such experiences may lead an adolescent to believe that he must remain in complete control in order to protect himself from painful personal feelings.

Parents and youth leaders can teach these young people that God is in charge and provides order to life, even when life does not seem kind or fair. Even when people fail us, God listens and cares. He is always bigger than our fears, our defeats, our pain. Thrash metal fans also need flesh-and-blood models of godly character—people who are both strong decision makers and compassionate listeners. These young fans can then see that God is not an enemy, nor is He an impotent wimp standing by while people suffer. If they will make room for Him, He will provide positive action in their lives.

Clues from Rap Music

Rap music reflects much of the same attitude as heavy metal. Macho posturing and street-corner bravado are very appealing to young teens, especially boys. Although many protest that they just like the beat, the pulsing lyrics of rap are driving home some strong and damaging messages about self-centered survival and quick-fix sex. While many rappers proudly say no to hard drugs, they still tend to glorify violence, gangs, crime, and life on the streets. Rap can feed the ego of insecure young teens who are in a hurry to be in complete control of their lives.

Parents and youth workers need to be willing to point out the errors in these philosophies promoting sex and violence. Young people need to be reminded that God created women for far greater potential and blessing than to be treated like prostitutes or sexual utensils. The arrogant boasting of many rappers is a poor, self-centered substitute for genuine self-esteem.

God has much better ways to help young people deal with insecurity and poor self-image. His grace and love are the solutions to a faltering heart. His plans for lasting, fulfilling relationships far exceed hit-and-run, instant, sexual gratification. His peace is the answer to gang conflict and rebellion against authority. If we can communicate these positive alternatives in a loving way, intelligent young people won't be fooled by the empty promises of rap music.

Clues from Pop/Dance Music

The sexuality of the pop/dance music of Madonna, Paula Abdul, and others tends to concern parents. But many young girls identify with this style of music. By doing so, they may be telling us that they fear they'll never be attractive or loved on their own merits. They may feel a need to act and look like the girls in the movies and music videos in order to get the attention they crave.

If a girl's father doesn't treat her as if

she is special, she's more likely to believe the musical myths of a song like George Michael's "Father Figure." She will cling to the promise that some guy will come along with just the right words to make her feel good about herself. It's surprising to find out how many attractive young ladies feel inadequate, ugly, and unloved.

God is a true Father figure who loves our daughters just the way they are. But they may need our help to realize what a special treasure they are in His sight. They need regular assurance of His perfect plan for their lives and of their parents' commitment of time, interest, and genuine caring—not just words. "Prove yourselves doers of the word, and not merely hearers who delude themselves" (James 1:22, NASB).

Are you beginning to see how your child's music can be a window to his soul? Young people consider their music to be an answer to some very real concerns. It addresses many of their personal and emotional needs. With a few good musical "clues," parents can begin to identify those needs. With prayer and wisdom, we can begin to provide solid, spiritual alternatives to the musical myths our children hear.

Parents, you must be prepared to be part of the answer yourselves. This healing process requires more than just saying the right words. You must put aside your own biases and anger. You must begin to minister as Jesus would minister. It's really not so hard to do when you don't have to put so much energy into wrestling the music monster. You have more freedom to listen and ask tender questions.

Keep in mind that your child's reaction will depend on your history of communication with him or her. Children might be defensive at first if they feel you are prying. Show a sincere interest, tempered with grace and mercy. Remember, you are asking them to reveal their innermost secrets, some of which they may never have tried to express before.

You can start this sensitive process by asking questions like these:

- *What are some of your favorite songs?*
- *Why does that song mean so much to you?*
- *Do you ever wonder whether you are going to grow up and survive?*
- *What are your views on sex and*

*love? Has your music helped shape
your views?*

- *Are you sometimes angry and
frustrated with this family?*

These are dangerous questions to ask if we
don't want to hear the truth. Do we have a
hard time admitting mistakes? Are we
afraid of our own inadequacies as parents?
Do we really have faith that God can handle
the situation? Do we feel comfortable being
vulnerable, open, honest, humble, and
emotional with our children? Even if this
experience is painful, it is necessary if we
are going to truly communicate with our
children. If we are going to find out where
they hurt, we need to find out what goes on
inside them.

Today's music speaks to our children. It
mirrors their souls. If we want to know the
hearts of our children, we must listen to
their music and discuss it with them.

DEALING WITH THE ISSUE

The question of what to do if a child listens
to rock music is certainly the one I hear most
often as I talk to parents and adults who
work with young people. I have agonized

over this issue—not only as a speaker, but also as a parent. These ideas are much more than theories to me. My staff and I have experimented, prayed, and searched diligently for the best biblical answers.

It is with confidence that we say the answers lie in treating your children as gifts from God whom you want to see conformed to the character of Christ. The desire to build positive communication within the family is the key. With these insights, we can begin to realistically respond to the problem of rock music with some hope of success. Let's look at a practical, step-by-step approach of dealing with rock music in the home.

1. Start on Your Knees.

So often when I say the first and best thing to do is to pray, I get a knowing look of smugness. I can tell that everyone is thinking, *Yes, of course, but what should I really do?*

What should we really do? Pray! We can't do anything more powerful or more effective than that. (See James 5:16.) We must not treat prayer as a spiritual cliché. God knows our concerns! He cares! He desires to hear from us. If Christian parents spent 30 minutes each day in fervent prayer for their children, do you believe their children would be different? If so, why aren't more of us doing it?

Every Christian intends to pray more than he actually does. Do you pray for your children every single day? Many parents pray with their children as they recite little rehearsed prayers at bedtime. But how often do you pray for them as they sleep or as you watch them go off to school? Do you regularly pray for their souls, for their futures, for their future spouses, and for their spiritual maturity?

I must confess that occasionally I start slipping in this important responsibility. I let the pressure of urgent deadlines force me into hurried prayers. But usually, before long, I am prompted by the Holy Spirit to remember how my mother prayed faithfully for me. She taught me that we may pray for our children for many years without seeing results, yet we must keep praying in obedience to the will of God.

When you're ready to deal with the issue of rock music, here are some prayer concerns you might want to consider:

- *Pray for wisdom and a loving attitude.*
- *Pray for patience to treat your children as gifts from your heavenly Father and to remember that they are not the problem.*
- *Pray that you'll be able to control your emotions during your discussions.*
- *Pray that you'll be able to give priority to the things God wants to teach them, giving the Holy Spirit room to do His work.*
- *Pray that your children will be open to these discussions.*
- *Pray that you and your children will be able to trust each other and listen to each other.*
- *Pray that you can effectively let them know that you care and understand.*
- *Pray for enhanced communications. The Lord promises to give us the right words to speak when we get into difficult situations (Matthew 10:19). Pray for the right words, believing God will fulfill His promise.*

2. Set Entertainment Guidelines for Your Family.

Sit down with your spouse and discuss your current and future entertainment guidelines. Be as honest and realistic as possible. Where do you stand? How much are you willing to tolerate? How much media do you want in your home? What kinds? What about records, tapes, CDs, radio, videos, TV? Will you allow rock posters on the walls? Is it okay to buy and read rock magazines? Do you want to set a daily limit on the amount of rock music or TV? Do you want restrictions on volume?

Pray about these guidelines and put them down in writing. Begin with what you think would be ideal. List what you are willing to put up with. You may want to discuss your guidelines with your pastor or youth director for additional feedback, especially if you are a single parent. Honestly evaluate whether these guidelines are fair to your children. Do they honestly reflect your faith? Are they biblical? Can you explain why? Make sure you can express your convictions in terms that everyone in the family can understand.

Parents may be tempted to enforce the limits they've set by sneaking into their children's rooms while the kids are at school and tossing out music that doesn't meet the guidelines. This action will *not* enhance family communications or glorify God. Children need to learn to make spiritual commitments for themselves. They need a model for arriving at spiritual decisions that they can understand and imitate.

Be prepared for a number of discussions. Do not try to accomplish everything in one meeting. You cannot discuss complex biblical issues regarding music, radio, TV, movies, magazines, and other forms of entertainment in one sitting. You will need to address these issues in bite-sized pieces that can be digested and acted on without causing major upheaval in the family structure. Remember, the goal is to draw the family closer to Christ and to each other, not just to lay down the law.

If you decide to eliminate some of the entertainment from your home, decide how to restructure the extra time you create. For instance, if your third grader is watching too many hours of cartoons on TV in the morning and you cut the amount in half, how can you replace those hours with constructive activity? It has to be something that the child considers interesting and meaningful. We cannot take away his TV time and then have him wash the dishes instead. Rather, find an option that will bring the family closer together and help the child understand how to glorify Jesus Christ.

Along with the guidelines, develop a predetermined course of action to help enforce them. How are you going to measure the limits set for TV viewing? How will you monitor music listening in the home? How are you going to respond if the guidelines are violated? How many warnings will your children be given? What if a *parent* violates the guidelines? Be prepared to explain and justify your responses.

Setting guidelines generally works best when the children are still preschool or in elementary school. Parents of these age groups have a lot of authority and the ability to guide their children in making spiritual decisions. The earlier you determine the parental limits in your home, the better it will be for your family.

3. Make Certain Your Act Is Together.

Have you honestly and biblically evaluated the entertainment areas of your own life? Have you set harder standards for your children than for yourself, or is the example consistent in your home?

Are both parents in clear agreement about the limits that were set? If you do not present a united front, your children will play one parent against the other to get what they want. But if the guidelines are well written, they will not be subject to the changing moods of a parent or child. Fair enforcement of the rules will be as much of a discipline for you as for your children.

This process is somewhat different for a single parent. If the other spouse is not involved in child rearing, then the active parent must do his or her best to enforce the guidelines alone. In many divorce situations, the other parent is still partly involved in child rearing through weekend parenting or summer custody. If you still have an amicable relationship, explain your guidelines and convictions. Try to come to an agreement so the child will be treated the same by both parents.

If, however, the other parent is not agreeable, still angry or hurting over the relationship, or a non-Christian, you have a more serious problem than music in your home (though music will often be the symptom of the unrest such a situation creates in your children's lives). If this is your situation, seek counseling for the real issues at hand, and pray that God will bring unity and salvation through these difficult circumstances.

4. Explain Your Guidelines to Your Children.

Sit down with your whole family and discuss the limits you have set. Meet around the kitchen table after dinner or on Saturday morning at breakfast. Turn off the TV and shut out other distractions. Tell your children of your convictions about the influences of music and entertainment. Be willing to concede that they might not understand or share your feelings, and be vulnerable enough to confess if you haven't been living up to the proposed standards yourself.

Share your earnest desire to live more consistently for God. Explain to your children that, like Daniel, you have purposed in your heart not to defile yourself with the "diet" the entertainment world offers (Daniel 1). Let them know that in your home, you intend to let your Christian principles and ethics determine which media are acceptable—no matter what other families are doing. State your reasons clearly.

Your children might not agree with all the limits you set, and they are likely to ask a lot of questions. They may see the proposed changes as punishment, rather than a rewarding experience. Be ready to give them biblical reasons for your decisions. Make sure they understand that you are not reacting out of fear or anger.

Be open-minded enough to listen to your children. Some of their complaints may be silly, immature, defiant, or spiritually foolish. But others may be legitimate excuses you never have thought of, personally important to the child because of peer pressure, school requirements, or any number of reasons. Children often have a simple wisdom that can keep us in balance.

Be prepared to bend a little, compromise, or even change some of the rules. Don't break your family because you're unwilling to bend. Love and respect your children enough to consider what they have to say. As the parents, you have the final word, but this cannot mean your children are to have no say whatsoever. As a family, put a plan together that is biblical, feasible, enforceable, and spiritually healthy.

Strive to give your children a sense of security, rather than a feeling of hysteria or dread. They may test the new guidelines to see if your resolve is serious. But when they understand where the limits are, they will feel more secure. This can be a rewarding, constructive process. It also gives your children an effective model by which to explain their entertainment choices to friends later on.

After everyone has discussed the new guidelines, prepare a written contract for the family. Write down how the family will evaluate and choose music, purchase tapes, watch television, and so forth. Put the result of your discussions in print and give each family member a copy.

For example, my wife and I do not allow our daughters to have secular music that teaches unbiblical philosophies. We allow them to listen to an occasional secular record that is inoffensive or biblically consistent, and they may buy one if they are willing to spend their own money on it. However, my daughters know I will buy any Christian music they want because I consider it an investment in their future spiritual growth.

Also, our family television viewing is based on Psalm 101:3, which says, "I will set no worthless thing before my eyes." We actually have that verse written in calligraphy on a card which sits on our TV. If a program's content is against biblical values, we won't let it come into our home through television. And this guideline doesn't change after the children go to bed. If it is wrong for them, it is also wrong for my wife and me.

Obviously, a discussion of guidelines usually works best in a home setting where both parents are Christians and where the children are young. In such an environment, these discussions can be warm, fun, and enlightening. Parents and children can both grow spiritually. And in the desire to please their parents, young children will often set stricter limits for themselves than what you would demand. They can experience the rewards of properly responding to the freedom and encouragement you give them.

However, many families do not fit the ideal situation. In those homes, some of these steps become a bit more difficult. You may be tempted to resist this discussion altogether with the excuse that you work too hard and need to relax in front of the tube. But it is essential to take these steps if you are truly concerned about the entertainment in your home.

5. Spend Time with Your Teens.

I once heard a policeman describe the arrest of a young man who was the leader of a group of Satan worshippers in Texas. The whole community was shocked by the arrest because the young man had appeared to be a clean-cut, exemplary citizen. He was getting straight A's in school and was involved in several social clubs, so his secret involvement in Satanism came as a complete surprise—especially to his mother.

The investigators went to his home to search for clues about his satanic involvement. They had to break down the door to his room because there was a lock on it. Only the young man had the key. The police found rock posters, demonic literature, a locker full of materials to use as an altar to Satan, and even tapes of a psychodrama in which the young man portrayed himself as being possessed by the devil.

His mother later confessed that she had not set foot in his room for more than three years. All his activities had gone unchecked because she had refused to become involved in his life. She thought that she was communicating to her son that she was giving him freedom. But what she really communicated was that she didn't care about him. The son's shocking lifestyle was allowed to become excessive because his mother was out of touch with what he was doing.

I've met parents who are proud of the fact that they don't have the slightest idea what kinds of music their children listen to. They boast that they don't know the difference between ZZ Top and the Four Tops. Not only are these parents out of touch, they are also giving the impression that they don't love their children.

What if you did something four, six, or even eight hours a day without your spouse expressing an interest in it—even in passing? You might come to believe that he or she doesn't care about you as a person. You might even doubt whether he or she really loves you. After investing valuable hours each day, the person who is supposed to love you doesn't even know what you're doing. Eventually, you would be likely to resent your spouse because of his or her lack of interest.

Now think. How much interest do you show in the things your child enjoys? The average American teenager spends two to six hours a day listening to music. Anything that consumes so much of their time must be pretty important to them. Yet some parents don't even have a clue what groups their children like. How sad! The implication is that the parents just don't care.

This attitude makes it easier for young people to justify their alienation from parents. After all, their parents haven't even taken the time to find out what's so important to them. But when parents truly show an interest in the things that interest young people—even rock music—their children will be more likely to expose true feelings, dreams, and desires.

Parents need to become acquainted with the music and TV habits of their children. Do the kids have a television, a VCR, or a radio in their room? What have they been watching and listening to? Do they watch horror movies or sexual movies when they get with their friends? What kinds of CDs and tapes do they have in their collection? What radio stations do they listen to? What are their favorite groups?

After you answer these questions, do some research on any of the groups that are new to you. (Our ministry can help you with this.) Begin building bridges by indicating that you can say something intelligent about your child's music—not just that it's satanic, awful, or disgusting. Real facts are effective tools in opening up communication with your children. When they see that you honestly know something about their music, they realize that you are truly interested in them and what goes on in their world. It is important to develop a rapport with your child about his music.

Remember, the biggest sacrifice God asks parents to make is the sacrifice of time. Good communication with your teenage children won't take place in a day, a week, or even a month. It can be a long, growing process.

6. Weed Out Unacceptable Entertainment.

After meeting as a family to discuss entertainment guidelines, move the discussion into your child's room to discuss each person's entertainment, one at a time. Survey the child's room in regard to wall decorations, stereos, radios, TVs, VCRs, tapes and records, and so forth. (It is better not to let the child accumulate all of these electronic toys. It's not much of a punishment option to restrict a child to a room equipped like a luxury hotel!)

Once a survey is made of the child's room, make specific applications to your guidelines. It might be a easier to start the discussions on the topic of television. Together, you can decide what programs to watch or not watch. Then discuss when the radio can be listened to, and what videos should be allowed on the VCR in the room. Later discussions can bring up the subject of rock music.

Talk to your child about his faith and joy. Are they everything he wants them to be? Is he questioning his salvation or the validity of the Bible? Does he wonder if God is real and if He really cares? Does he exhibit the fruit of the spirit in his life—love, joy, peace, and so forth (Galatians 5:22, 23)? Has he ever struggled with thoughts of suicide? Is he feeling depressed or negative? How does he handle negative feelings? What does his music mean to him? Is it a primary means of escape?

Remain alert to the possibility that your children may not be genuinely saved. (You may come to that conclusion as you talk with them.) If this is the case, consider being less strict on the rock music issue. Your main concern shouldn't be their listening habits; it should be the condition of their soul. Begin to deal with issues like music, discipline, and school with a focus on how you can help your children come to know Christ.

With your child still in the room with you, examine his records, CDs, and tapes—group by group. What are the philosophies of these musicians and how do they compare with what Jesus teaches? Ask if the music encourages him to focus on things above instead rather than earthly things (Colossians 3:2).

You might ask a younger child, "Do the singers love Jesus?" If the child is older, you can ask, "Does the music encourage spiritual growth in your life?" If the child answers no, ask, "Can you afford to be influenced by this group?" If the child answers yes, ask, "*How* is the music helping you grow spiritually?"

Asking these questions shifts the burden of responsibility from your shoulders to his. It is left to him to make a positive decision. You no longer need to be your child's judge. If his answers satisfy you, thank God for your child's wisdom and maturity. Use this time to draw closer to your child and express the faith you hold together.

These may be difficult questions for your child to answer. He might respond, "I don't know," and shrug a lot. Press for real answers to your questions about his spiritual condition. Be patient and wait for specific answers to your specific questions. Here are some excuses I suggest you don't accept:

- *"I don't listen to the words!"*—Just play one of the child's favorite records and see how easily he remembers the lyrics. The child may not realize it, but his subconscious mind is fully aware of what's being sung.

- *"It doesn't affect me!"*—How can he be certain? If his faith and joy aren't strong, his entertainment could be a major influence.
- *"The musicians are only performing (immoral music) for the fun, money, and/or fame!"*—Who cares why they do it? The point is that their music is being produced and bought. Even if their motives aren't evil, the results on the listener may be!
- *"I don't listen to evil (or satanic) music."*—Have the child define evil. The majority of secular music promotes philosophies that are against biblical values. Doesn't it make more sense to listen to music that ministers, instead of music that is merely inoffensive?

Your children probably won't want to analyze their music. They just want to enjoy it. But push them gently and firmly toward the process of evaluating what they listen to. Help them investigate the possibility that their music contributes to their lack of spiritual growth, their discontent with the church, their irritation by friends in certain relationships, or other problems they may be facing. Their music may be giving them ideas that are creating or exaggerating these problems.

It isn't wise to start by throwing out your child's entire music collection. But remove offensive groups as you find them, and explain why you are doing so. Start with the worst music first and move to the middle ground. Don't take away undesirable music without offering something to take its place. Are you willing to substitute better records for the rock music you take away?

I suggest that you offer to replace the most offensive records with Christian music. In addition to providing entertainment, Christian music is a valuable tool to help a believer focus on life from God's point of view. Used effectively, it can strengthen your child's spiritual life.

Before you recoil at the potential

expense of exchanging a Christian record-
ing for every offensive record, tape, or CD
in your child's collection, think of it as an
investment. Investments may be expensive,
but they return dividends. I believe you'll
see the dividends in your child as he grows
in the Lord through the influence and
encouragement of Christian music.

Christian music is available in almost
every music style. If you don't know what
Christian music artists to substitute for your
child's groups, go to your local Christian
bookstore. Many have listening centers that
will allow you to sample a wide variety.
Also, feel free to contact our office.

7. Reevaluate Your Guidelines.

Parents often discover that discussions with
children prove to be quite revealing—even
surprising. Adults usually have specific
expectations about the child's condition
and what needs to be done. But after
actually talking and listening to their
children, many parents find that the
situation is completely different than they
expected.

Parents may need to renegotiate the
contract, set new limits, or alter the

standards according to what they discover. Some parents will find that their children are more deeply involved in secular music than they believed possible. Others will find that their children are much more mature than they had realized. It's amazing how quickly we can get out of touch with our children's lives.

Don't compromise your spiritual and family values, but don't be stubborn either. Be willing to adjust and reset limits that will be most constructive for the child. You don't need to settle these complex issues overnight. Children grow gradually, so don't panic. God is in control. Show that you trust Him, and make it clear that you want to trust your children, too.

Before I had children, I thought I had all the answers. Now I realize some boundaries are open for discussion and others are firm. R-rated movies, immoral television programs, and music opposed to biblical values are not open for discussion. Other decisions are. If I don't learn to bend in nonessentials, I am likely to break any positive relationship I might ever have with my children.

Let me share an example of what I

mean. Originally, when we set up guide-lines with our daughters, we decided they would include only Christian posters in their bedrooms. One day I noticed my older daughter had a picture on her wall of a cute young man who starred in a television show our family watched regularly. Although he was a clean-cut, nice young man, the picture didn't fit in the guideline we had set.

Should I make her take it down or should I bend my limits? After a healthy discussion, we chose to include moral, clean-cut guys in our revised limits. Did I capitulate and allow my daughter to control me? I don't believe so. I decided to bend to prevent my relationship with my daughter from breaking. The important thing is that we talked it out and kept our relationship open.

The key to goal setting is to put goals into bite-sized chunks—steps that are easily achievable. Give children these kinds of goals. If a child has two hundred records, he probably isn't going to want to throw them out by tomorrow. Discuss the music, group by group and record by record, until you have a collection that reflects the limitations you've set in the home. Freely admit your mistake if you find that you misjudged a group or if you heard a rumor that turned out to be untrue. Being honest is not the same as being wishy-washy.

The ultimate goal in this entire process should be to strengthen our faith and joy, to open up communication within the family, and to help our kids become strong Christians who reflect the character and love of Christ.

WHAT TO THINK OR HOW TO THINK?

We need to teach our kids that we desire to serve Christ and to be unified as a family. We also want to teach them how to make spiritual decisions for themselves. Parents must let go of the reins little by little, whether they are ready or not. The most difficult thing for a parent to do is watch growth in their children occur slowly.

A major frustration many of us have about teaching Christian values is waiting for the child to accept what we say. We know from experience that we are right! We know Jesus Christ is God. We believe the Bible is true—every word. We know there is no other way to salvation than through

Jesus. We are saved by grace through His shed blood.

These are the very basics of our belief. And because we know the truth, it is often difficult not to give our children all the answers. In fact, when they resist, we want to force the truth on them. After all, we *know* we are right. If we don't give them the right answers, they might never find them.

But would you send your child to a school that gave tests with all the answers already filled in? What if your child only had to sign his name on the test to get an "A"? At such a school your child would never learn to think and solve problems on his own.

And yet, this is what is happening in many Christian homes, churches, and schools across the country. Parents are filling in all the answers for their children's questions about life, God, and Christianity. The children aren't taught to search the Scriptures and learn for themselves. They aren't trained to think critically and discover right from wrong. They aren't allowed to make decisions for themselves.

Many decisions are being made for young people without discussion or explanation—"Just sign your name." And we are quick to label those who won't "sign" as troublemakers. Maybe your troublemaker is simply expressing frustration at not being allowed to think for himself!

Too often in the church we have taught our kids *what* to think, not *how* to think. Churches are full of young people who recite all the right answers and look like "good Christians" on the outside. We have given them all the answers, told them what to do, and dictated how they should live. But we haven't told them how to discern truth through Scripture, how to serve Christ, or how to make good decisions.

When these children leave home, we might have filled in the answers for issues A, B, and C. But if the world throws something new at them, they have no idea how to respond. Why? We've spent too much time getting them to conform to our desires instead of helping them discover God's!

A former student of mine had parents who kept her on a tight rein. She was allowed to make very few decisions—even on little things. Outwardly, she looked like the perfect child. She got good grades, had lots of friends, and never got into trouble.

But later, as an adult, life became quite different for her. She is on her third husband, she has alienated herself from her former school friends and family, and is very antagonistic toward the things of Christ. In fact, she is very vocal in her radical, liberal beliefs.

As I think back to her school years, I remember that she was afraid to express herself. She was never taught to think spiritually on her own. Now that she no longer has the restraint of her parents, she freely expresses the anger and hatred that have been bottled up for years. She sees no purpose for Christianity except as a set of rules to keep people like her in line. Her parents still don't understand that her rebellion just might have something to do with her legalistic upbringing.

Parents, how many times have you seen this same scenario take place at your church or even in your own home? Do you know people who know the truth of the Gospel and try to force it down their children's throats? As many as 70% or more children raised by Christian parents never live for Jesus Christ as adults. We must begin teaching our children *how* to think instead of merely telling them *what* to think.

We don't help our children if we just dictate which musical groups to listen to, which records to buy, and which movies to watch. We need to set guidelines and show them how to make these decisions for themselves. If we are loving and patient as we work with them, they are more likely to desire God and seek *His* answers for their questions. After all, that's the *real* goal of dealing with rock music in our children's lives.

"Do not provoke your children to anger; but bring them up in the discipline and instruction of the Lord" (Ephesians 6:4).

Helping Families Grow Series

❦ *Communicating Spiritual Values Through Christian Music*

❦ *Equipping Your Child for Spiritual Warfare*

❦ *Family Vacations that Work*

❦ *Helping Your Child Stand Up to Peer Pressure*

❦ *How to Discover Your Child's Unique Gifts*

❦ *How to Work With Your Child's Teachers*

❦ *Helping Your Child Love to Read*

❦ *Improving Your Child's Self-Image*

❦ *Preparing for Your New Baby*

❦ *Should My Child Listen to Rock Music?*

❦ *Spiritual Growth Begins At Home*

❦ *Surviving the Terrible Teenage Years*